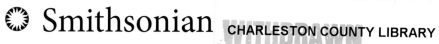

The Secrets of JUPITER

by Thomas K. Adamson

CAPSTONE PRESS
a capstone imprint

Capstone Press
1710 Roe Crest Drive, North Mankato, Minnesota 56003
www.capstonepub.com

Library of Congress Cataloging-in-Publication Data
Adamson, Thomas K.–author.
  The secrets of Jupiter / by Thomas K. Adamson.
    pages cm. — (Smithsonian. Planets)
  Includes index.
  Summary: "Discusses the planet Jupiter, including observations by ancient cultures, current knowledge of Jupiter, and plans for future scientific research and space exploration"—Provided by publisher.
  Audience: Ages 8-10
  Audience: Grades 2 to 4
  ISBN 978-1-4914-5864-8 (library binding)
  ISBN 978-1-4914-5897-6 (paperback)
  ISBN 978-1-4914-5908-9 (eBook PDF)
1. Jupiter (Planet)—Juvenile literature. 2. Jupiter (Planet)—Exploration—Juvenile literature. I. Title.
  QB661.A34 2016
  523.45—dc23   2014046199

Editorial Credits
Elizabeth R. Johnson, editor; Tracy Davies McCabe and Kazuko Collins, designers;
Wanda Winch, media researcher; Tori Abraham, production specialist

Our very special thanks to Andrew K. Johnston, Geographer, Center for Earth and Planetary Studies, National Air and Space Museum, Smithsonian Institution, for his curatorial review. Capstone would also like to thank Kealy Gordon, Smithsonian Institution Product Development Manager, and the following at Smithsonian Enterprises: Ellen Nanney, Licensing Manager; Brigid Ferraro, Director of Licensing; Carol LeBlanc, Senior Vice President, Consumer & Education Products; Chris Liedel, President.

Photo Credits
Black Cat Studios: Ron Miller, 12, 13, 17; Capstone, 7 (top); European Space Agency, 22 (right); Library of Congress: Prints and Photographs Division, 9 (top); Lunar and Planetary Institute, 5 (back), 11; NASA, 24, JPL, 15, 22 (Left), 23 (left), JPL-Caltech, 18, 23 (right), 29, JPL/Courtesy of Steve Vance, 19 (front), JPL/University of Arizona, cover, back cover, 1, 5 (back), 16, Michael Carroll, 21, MIT/H. Hammel, 27, NSSDC Photo Gallery, 19 (back), Planetary Photojournal, 9 (bottom); Shutterstock: Astrostar, space background, Dennis van de Water, 7 (bottom), Stephen Girimont, 25

Direct Quotations
Page 19 from interview with Reuters published May 2, 2014, www.reuters.com

Printed in the United States of America.
009988R

Table of Contents

Giant Planet

Jupiter is the true giant among the planets in our solar system. It is more massive than all of the other planets put together. It has the largest moon of any planet and huge storms that last for years.

As the biggest planet, Jupiter might hold the biggest mysteries. The planet's colorful clouds hide what's inside.

Jupiter has many moons. At least one of its large moons might have water under its icy surface. It's even possible that life may exist there.

Jupiter is 11 times wider than Earth. If Earth were as wide as a quarter, Jupiter would be a dinner plate.

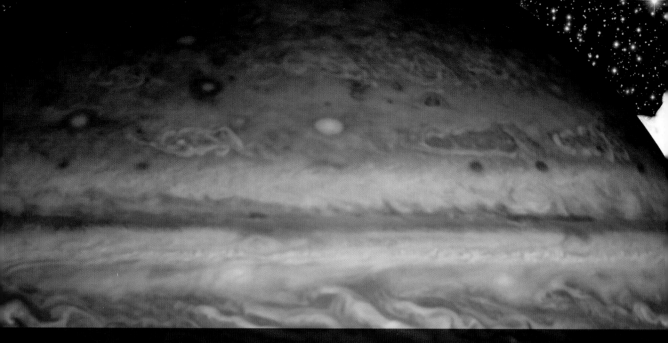

Fast Facts

Distance from Sun: 484 million miles
(779 million kilometers)

Diameter: 86,881 miles
(139,821 km)

Moons: at least 67

Rings: 4

Length of day: 10 hours

Length of year: 12 Earth years

Earth

Jupiter

Spying Jupiter

When Jupiter is in the night sky, it's hard to miss. It looks like a really bright star. Only the Sun, Moon, and Venus are brighter. Features of Jupiter and its large moons are visible with a small telescope or binoculars.

Jupiter's existence has never been a secret. Ancient people watched the night sky. The stars stayed in the same positions. Other points of light seemed to wander night after night. These were planets. Jupiter was always one of the brightest.

The planet was named after the most important god to the ancient Greeks and Romans. For the Greeks, it was Zeus. The Romans called it Jupiter.

Oppositions

Earth moves around the Sun faster than Jupiter does. Earth catches up to Jupiter about every 13 months. When Earth passes Jupiter in its orbit, Jupiter and the Sun are on opposite sides of Earth. This event is called an opposition. Oppositions are great times to observe Jupiter because it will be high in the sky when it's really dark.

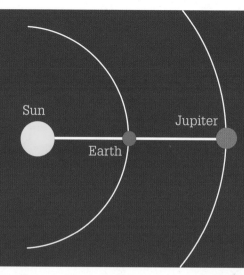

Galileo Reveals a Secret

Ancient people could not observe the planets and stars with much detail. Based on what they saw, they thought the stars, Sun, Moon, and planets moved around Earth.

Astronomer Nicolaus Copernicus proposed the heliocentric model of the universe in 1514. It stated that the Sun was the center of the universe and that planets moved around it instead of around Earth. This was a startling change in how people viewed the universe.

Galileo Galilei made a discovery that supported Copernicus' theory in 1610. He used a telescope he had built himself to look at the night sky. Some of the most important things he observed were the four moons moving around Jupiter. They changed positions every night. He discovered that there were objects going around something besides Earth. This was clear proof that Earth was not the center of the solar system.

Galileo was from Italy. He studied math and built his own telescope. In addition to Jupiter's moons, he was also the first person to see and note the rugged mountains and craters on Earth's moon. Through his telescope, Galileo also discovered Saturn's rings.

The four moons that Galileo observed are Jupiter's largest moons. They are known as the Galilean moons because of his important discovery.

Jupiter's Beginning

Long ago, when the planets were forming, the gases hydrogen, helium, ammonia, and methane were common. Far from the Sun, it was extremely cold. These gases turned into icy bits. The icy bits swirled and stuck together.

Over time the bits got big enough to attract more gas and dust. Gravity pulled the heavier material toward the center of each forming planet. The lighter gases stayed in the atmosphere.

Closer to the Sun, solar wind blew most of these gases away from the smaller rocky planets such as Earth. Farther from the Sun, the cold gases stayed around the forming planets. Jupiter and the other gas giants (Saturn, Uranus, and Neptune) were able to grow very big.

The gas giants all spin quickly, but none faster than Jupiter. The huge planet completes one spin, or one day, every 10 hours. Earth's spin takes 24 hours.

Number of Earths that could fit inside Jupiter: 1,321

Jupiter's Gases

Jupiter's fast spin swirls its clouds into colorful patterns. Gases move up and down in Jupiter's atmosphere. The bright colors are gases rising into the atmosphere. The dark colors are gas moving down toward the planet's interior.

Jupiter is made of gases—mostly hydrogen and helium. This planet has a core but no solid surface on which you could walk.

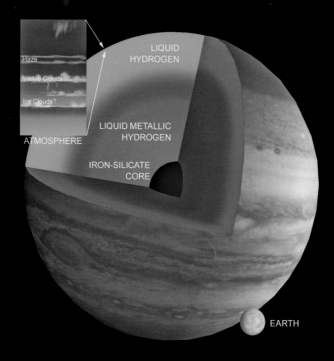

Scientists are still not sure if Jupiter's core is made of molten or solid rock—it's still a secret!

Temperatures get hotter as you move inward toward the core. The top of the atmosphere is a very cold -261 degrees Fahrenheit (-163 °C). The center of the planet is more than 43,000 miles (69,000 km) from the surface. At only 93 miles (150 km) down, the temperature is already about 260 °F (127 °C).

artist illustration of Jupiter's atmosphere

If you could go down into Jupiter's atmosphere, you would see it change from a gas to a liquid. Closer in it becomes a strange thick liquid made of metal hydrogen. Think of it as hydrogen soup. Temperatures there are hotter than the Sun's surface.

Jupiter's Mysterious Storms

The Great Red Spot is a huge storm on Jupiter. This spinning storm is bigger than Earth. People have known about this storm for as long as we have been observing Jupiter with telescopes. But it's still a big mystery. Scientists don't know why it's red, how it can last so long, or why it's there at all.

A large white storm got close to the Great Red Spot in 2000. Five years later the white spot also turned red. It's about half the size of the larger storm. Astronomers named it Red Spot Jr.

Other smaller storms have appeared and disappeared over the years. But the Great Red Spot continues to storm.

The Great Shrinking Red Spot?

The Great Red Spot has been shrinking since the 1930s.
In 2014 the Hubble Space Telescope took a picture of Jupiter.
It showed the spot as the smallest it has ever been measured.
Astronomers don't know if the shrinking will continue. Maybe
the famous, mysterious storm will die out someday.

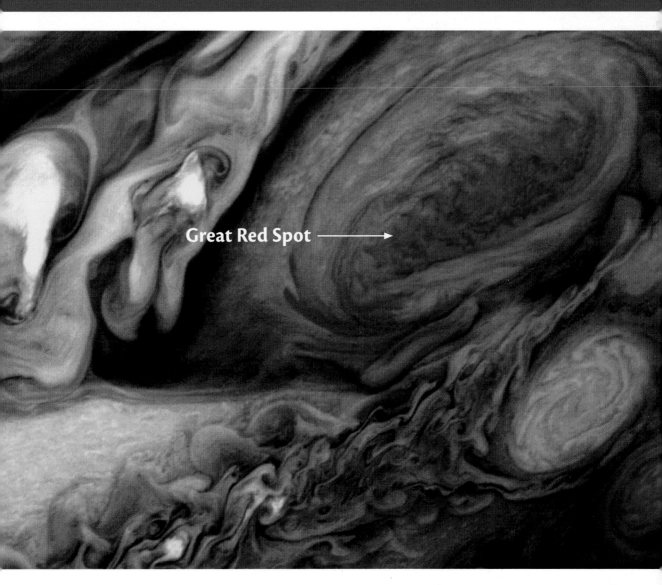

Great Red Spot ⟶

Big Galilean Moons Hold Big Secrets

Jupiter's Galilean moons are some of the weirdest places in space. The moon Io looks like a pizza you wouldn't want to eat. Geysers shoot sulfur dioxide gas high above the surface. Some of the lava from the geysers is hotter than lava on Earth.

Why is Io so hot?

The gravity from Jupiter and Jupiter's other moons pulls on Io from different directions. It squeezes and releases the moon over and over, creating heat that keeps Io's interior warm. The same thing might be happening at the moon Europa, warming liquid water under the icy surface.

While Io is hot, the moon Europa is covered by ice. It looks like the ice in Earth's Arctic Sea, covered in cracks and ridges. The ice may be floating on a liquid ocean.

The view from Io would show a sky one-fourth filled with giant Jupiter.

artist illustration of Europa

Europa might have more water than Earth.

This liquid ocean might be the most exciting of Jupiter's secrets. The presence of water means that life could possibly exist in there. Europa might be one of the most likely places other than Earth for life to exist. But scientists don't know how thick the icy shell is. They don't know what kind of life could be there. It could be microscopic or it could be similar to the organisms that live on Earth's deep ocean floor. Or it might not exist at all.

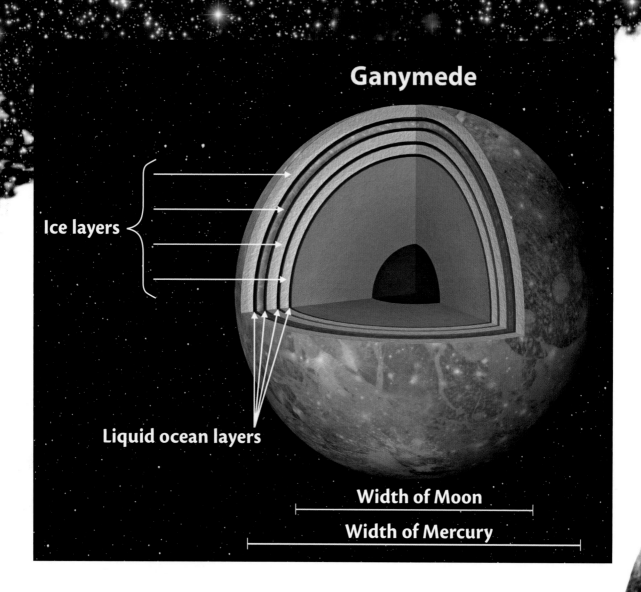

Ganymede

Ice layers

Liquid ocean layers

Width of Moon

Width of Mercury

The Galilean moons Ganymede and Callisto are both made of rock covered with ice. The ice on both moons is heavily spotted with craters. The moons also might have slushy liquid under the ice.

Ganymede is the biggest moon in the solar system. It's even bigger than Mercury. Scientists think that Ganymede may have multiple layers of ice, water, slush, and dense ice. As with Europa, it's possible that life could exist in the water layer. Missions to all of the Galilean moons will be needed to learn more about these mysteries.

Scientist Spotlight: Steve Vance

Steve Vance is a planetary scientist and astrobiologist. That means he studies planets and moons and whether they might have life. He led a team that did experiments in a lab with water, salt, and ice. It was this team that uncovered the secret of Ganymede's layers. Vance compared the moon's interior to a club sandwich. "That would make it the largest club sandwich in the solar system," Vance joked. Their experiment also supports the idea that there may be liquid water and perhaps even life under Ganymede's ice.

Callisto

Small Moons

Besides the four Galilean moons, Jupiter has dozens of small moons. Most of them go around Jupiter in the opposite direction that Jupiter rotates. This kind of orbit is not typical and is called retrograde. This leads astronomers to think that they are asteroids that Jupiter captured.

Moons that form at the same time that the planet forms generally orbit in the same direction. Moons that have a retrograde orbit are usually asteroids that traveled into the planet's gravitational field and were captured.

The largest of these small moons are Himalia and Amalthea. The rest of Jupiter's small moons range in size from 104 miles (167 km) to 0.6 miles (1 km) across.

Jupiter's moons are all named for characters in Greek and Roman mythology that are related to Zeus or Jupiter.

Naming Moons

When a moon is discovered, it gets a temporary name, such as S/2011 J2. The S stands for satellite. Next is the year it was discovered: 2011. The J stands for Jupiter. S/2011 J2 was the second moon of Jupiter discovered that year. That's why it's J2. After astronomers determine the moon's orbit more accurately, it gets a real name assigned by an international group of astronomers.

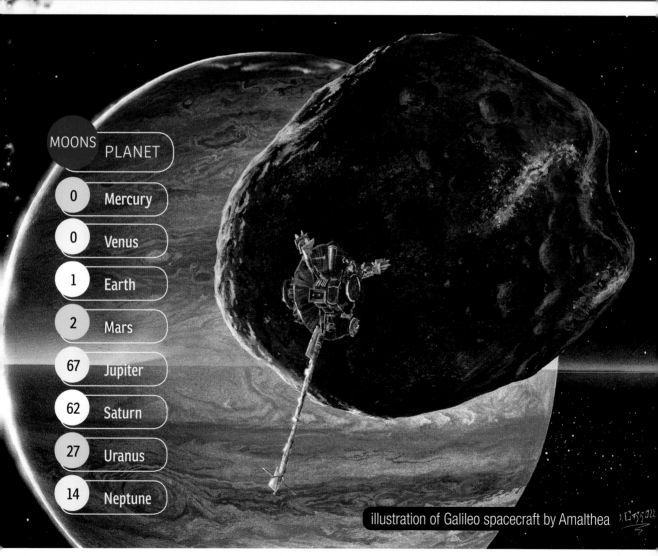

MOONS	PLANET
0	Mercury
0	Venus
1	Earth
2	Mars
67	Jupiter
62	Saturn
27	Uranus
14	Neptune

illustration of Galileo spacecraft by Amalthea

Visitors to Jupiter

Several spacecraft have gotten up-close looks at Jupiter over the years.

Timeline

1973—Pioneer 10 is the first spacecraft to fly by Jupiter.

1974—Pioneer 11 flies by Jupiter.

March 1979—Voyager 1 discovers Io's geysers and shows Jupiter's thin rings.

The rings are very thin and dark and barely visible. The rings each have a small moon near them. The rings may have formed from pieces that broke off these tiny moons.

Voyager 2

July 1979—Voyager 2 reveals the strange cracks in Europa's ice. Photos of Io show that its surface has changed since Voyager 1's visit.

1992—Ulysses uses Jupiter to get into a polar orbit around the Sun.

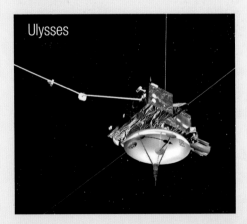
Ulysses

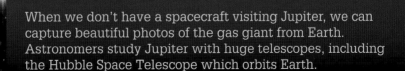

When we don't have a spacecraft visiting Jupiter, we can capture beautiful photos of the gas giant from Earth. Astronomers study Jupiter with huge telescopes, including the Hubble Space Telescope which orbits Earth.

2000—Cassini flies by Jupiter; Jupiter's gravity helps Cassini speed up and get to Saturn.

Cassini

1995–2003—Galileo orbits Jupiter and collects information about Jupiter and its moons.

2007—New Horizons takes pictures of Red Spot Jr. on its way to Pluto. It also takes more pictures of Io's geysers. It spots a gigantic plume pouring out of a volcano called Tvashtar.

2016—Juno is scheduled to reach Jupiter.

Juno

Galileo was the first spacecraft to orbit Jupiter.
It arrived in 1995 and orbited the planet until 2003.
Galileo flew close to Europa. Its observations support
the idea that there is water underneath its icy surface.

Galileo also dropped a probe into Jupiter's
atmosphere. A parachute slowed the probe as it
plunged 97 miles (156 km) into Jupiter's atmosphere.
It measured winds and gases. The probe survived
for almost one hour and then was crushed by the
pressure of Jupiter's atmosphere.

Galileo drops the probe

artist illustration of Galileo

Comet Collision: A Secret in Real Time

Comet Shoemaker-Levy 9 was discovered in 1993. Astronomers soon learned that it was on a collision course with Jupiter. It was the first observed collision of two solar system bodies. Jupiter's gravity broke the comet into 21 pieces. Those pieces slammed into Jupiter in July 1994. The impacts had the strength of 300 gigatons of TNT. The scars from the impacts were visible for nearly a year.

Gigaton
a unit of explosive force equal to 1 billion tons of trinitrotoluene (TNT)

Jupiter acts like the vacuum cleaner of the solar system. Its huge size and strong gravity draw small objects toward it. So Jupiter cleans up the solar system's debris. These types of collisions have happened before but had never been seen. In a photo of Ganymede, a chain of craters can be seen across the surface. The craters were likely caused by a collision similar to Shoemaker-Levy 9.

impact scar from Shoemaker-Levy 9

The most spectacular photos of the collision were from the Hubble Space Telescope. The collision happened on the side of Jupiter facing away from Earth. But as Jupiter rotated, the impact scars came into view. Jupiter's winds eventually wiped out the marks.

Another collision with Jupiter happened in 2009. This time it was something smaller. Scientists believe it might have been an asteroid. The Hubble telescope took impressive shots of the scars caused by this collision too.

Juno Looks for Answers

More secrets about Jupiter may soon be revealed. A new spacecraft called Juno reaches Jupiter in 2016. Juno is NASA's first solar-powered spacecraft designed to travel such great distances. In order for Juno to capture enough sunlight so far from the Sun, the solar panels stretch out to make the spacecraft about 66 feet (20 meters) wide.

Juno will send back information about how the atmosphere moves deep under Jupiter's cloud tops. Juno will also find out how much water is in Jupiter's atmosphere. This will give scientists clues about how Jupiter and other planets formed. What they learn can even help them learn about how planets form around other stars besides the Sun.

In Roman mythology Jupiter placed clouds around himself to hide his mischief. His wife, Juno, could see through the clouds and see what he was up to. The Juno spacecraft will also look beneath the planet's clouds.

artist illustration of Juno

Jupiter is the largest planet in our solar system and people have known about it for thousands of years. But it still holds plenty of secrets. Could there be life under the ice of its large moons? Does a solid core exist under all that gas? Will the Great Red Spot disappear someday? Scientists keep working to unlock these mysteries.

Glossary

asteroid (AS-tuh-royd)—a small, rocky body that orbits the Sun

atmosphere (AT-muhss-fihr)—the mixture of gases that surrounds a planet or moon

comet (KAH-mit)—a rock that goes around the Sun in a long, slow path; when close to the Sun, it has a long tail of light

crater (KRAY-tuhr)—a large hole in the ground caused by something such as a bomb or meteorite

geyser (GYE-zur)—an underground spring that shoots water, steam, or other material into the air

gravity (GRAV-uh-tee)—the force that pulls things down or to the center of a planet and keeps them from floating away into space

Hubble Space Telescope (HUHB-uhl)—the telescope that orbits Earth in space; it allows scientists to study faraway objects in space or other planets in the solar system

molten (MOHLT-uhn)—melted by heat; lava is molten rock

mythology (mih-THAH-luh-jee)—a group of myths or stories that belong to a culture

observation (ahb-zur-VAY-shuhn)—something you have noticed by watching carefully

orbit (OR-bit)—the invisible path followed by an object circling a planet, the Sun, etc.

polar orbit (POH-lur)—an orbital path that goes around a planet or star from north pole to south pole, rather than around the equator

probe (PROHB)—a tool or device used to explore or examine something, as in a space probe

retrograde (REH-truh-greyd)—having a backward motion or direction

satellite (SAT-uh-lite)—an object, natural or man-made, orbiting a planet or a moon

Read More

Chiger, Arielle, and Elkin, Matthew. *20 Fun Facts about Gas Giants.*
Fun Fact File: Space! New York: Gareth Stevens, 2015.

Nardo, Don. *Destined for Space: Our Story of Exploration.* Mankato,
Minn: Capstone Press, 2012.

Owen, Ruth. *Jupiter.* Explore outer space. New York:
Windmill Books, 2014.

Internet Sites

FactHound offers a safe, fun way to find Internet sites related to
this book. All of the sites on FactHound have been researched by
our staff.

Here's all you do:

Visit *www.facthound.com*

Type in this code: 9781491458648

FactHound will fetch the best sites for you!

Super-cool stuff! Check out projects, games and lots more at
www.capstonekids.com

Critical Thinking Using the Common Core

1. Read the sidebar on page 7. When is the best time to see Jupiter in the night sky? Why? (Key Ideas and Details)

2. Read the text on page 28 and look at the illustration on page 29. Why are Juno's solar panels so big? What does that tell you about the amount of heat Jupiter receives from the Sun? (Integration of Knowledge and Ideas)

Index